Y 616.951 BYE
Byers, Ann.
Sexually transmitted diseases :

NOV 6 2001

**HENRY COUNTY
LIBRARY SYSTEM**
DATE DUE
MAY 2 1 2002

LOCUST GROVE PUBLIC LIBRARY
115 LOCUST GROVE-GRIFFIN ROAD
LOCUST GROVE, GA 30248

Sexually Transmitted Diseases

A Hot Issue

Ann Byers

Enslow Publishers, Inc.
40 Industrial Road
Box 398
Berkeley Heights, NJ 07922
USA

PO Box 38
Aldershot
Hants GU12 6BP
UK

http://www.enslow.com

Copyright © 1999 by Enslow Publishers, Inc.

All rights reserved.

No part of this book may be reproduced by any means without the written permission of the publisher.

Library of Congress Cataloging-in-Publication Data

Byers, Ann.
    Sexually transmitted diseases : a hot issue / Ann Byers.
       p. cm. — (Hot issues)
    Includes bibliographical references and index.
    Summary: Describes different kinds of sexually transmitted diseases, including gonorrhea, syphilis, chlamydia, pelvic inflammatory disease, herpes, hepatitis, and AIDS, explaining how they are transmitted, how they manifest themselves, and how they can be avoided or treated.
    ISBN 0-7660-1192-5
    1. Sexually transmitted diseases—Juvenile literature.
[1. Sexually transmitted diseases. 2. Diseases.]
I. Title. II. Series.
RC200.25.B94   1999
616.95'1—dc21   98-44420
                                                                           CIP
                                                                           AC

Printed in the United States of America

10 9 8 7 6 5 4 3 2 1

To Our Readers:
All Internet addresses in this book were active and appropriate when we went to press. Any comments or suggestions can be sent by e-mail to Comments@enslow.com or to the address on the back cover.

Illustration Credits: Enslow Publishers, Inc., p. 13; © The Stock Market/Lightscapes, 1995, p. 52; © 1995 The Stock Market/Ted Horowitz, p. 11; © Corel Corporation, pp. 1, 4, 6, 24, 30, 33, 48; U.S. Department of Health and Human Services, Public Health Service, Centers for Disease Control and Prevention (CDC), *STD Surveillance 1997*, September 1998: Reproduced by Enslow Publishers, Inc., pp. 36, 38, 40.

Cover Illustration: © Corel Corporation

Contents

Introduction.................... 4

1 Hidden Epidemic: What STDs Are All About.................... 7

2 Paying the Piper: Consequences of STDs.................... 16

3 The (SE)X Generation: Who Gets STDs?.................... 26

4 Types of Infection: The Diseases.................... 34

5 After the Party: What Should People With STDs Do?.................... 45

6 Taking Charge: How to Prevent STDs.................... 51

Where to Find Help.................... 56

Chapter Notes.................... 57

Glossary.................... 61

Further Reading.................... 63

Index.................... 64

Introduction

Michelle did not think twice about having sex. She really liked Joe. She was young, just ready to begin college, her whole life ahead of her.

But in that single act of intercourse, Joe gave Michelle more than a "good time." He gave her a painful disease.

For weeks, Michelle was unaware that an infection was growing inside her body. After awhile, she began to have terrible stomach cramps and her menstrual periods became irregular. But she ignored the pains and the unusual bleeding for months.

When she finally sought medical attention, the doctor did not think Michelle's complaints were serious. But they were. By the time physicians realized that Michelle was suffering from pelvic inflammatory disease (PID), she almost died. It took two weeks in a hospital and massive amounts of antibiotics to save her life.

Even then, the disease was not gone. It came back—not once, but seven times. And it left her ovaries, her fallopian tubes, and her entire reproductive tract a jumble of scars. Several operations were necessary to repair some of the damage. But everything could not be mended and Michelle is unable to conceive or to bear children.[1]

Michelle is a real person. All the people whose stories are in this book are real. Their names have

Introduction

been changed to protect their privacy, but the trouble and hurt they experienced are genuine.

Sexually transmitted diseases (STDs) happen to real people. Some cause only minor discomfort; others bring excruciating pain. Some can be cured easily; others remain for life. Some lead to blindness, heart problems, or brain damage. Some can keep men as well as women from ever having children. Some end in death. All are preventable.

Number of New STD Cases in 1997 in the United States	
Chlamydia	526,653
Gonorrhea	324,901
Genital Warts	140,000*
PID	251,000*
Genital Herpes	175,000*
Syphilis	46,537
HIV/AIDS	14,515/60,634

*Approximate number

Sources: U.S. Department of Health and Human Services, Public Health Service, Centers for Disease Control and Prevention (CDC), *Sexually Transmitted Disease Surveillance 1997*, September 1998.

U.S. Department of Health and Human Services, Public Health Service, Centers for Disease Control and Prevention (CDC), *HIV/AIDS Surveillance Report*, Vol. 9, No. 2, December 1997.

*S*exually transmitted diseases are a concern for young people.

Chapter 1

Hidden Epidemic: What STDs Are All About

Our world is full of germs, tiny organisms too small to be seen by the human eye. Many are helpful, even necessary to life. Others cause disease when they get inside the human body.

Microorganisms, also called microbes, can get into the body through any opening: the nose, the mouth, a cut or sore where the skin is broken. Sexually transmitted diseases get into the body through openings in the sexual organs. These microscopic germs are transmitted, or passed, from one person to another when the microbes from the body of an infected person enter the body of a noninfected person. Anyone with disease-causing microbes in his or her genital area can pass those germs to another person by having sexual relations.

The Diseases

Sexually transmitted diseases (STDs) are infections that are caught through vaginal intercourse or through anal (rectal) or oral (mouth) sex. The microbes that cause the infections are usually passed in body fluids, especially semen from a male, vaginal fluid from a female, and blood. Some are transmitted by intimate skin-to-skin contact.

More than twenty-five different STDs are known to infect people today.[1] The most common ones are

- *Gonorrhea* and *syphilis*, the oldest known sexually transmitted diseases
- *Chlamydia*, the most prevalent bacterial STD in the United States
- *Pelvic inflammatory disease (PID)*, which affects only women and is the result of some other sexual infection that is not treated
- *Herpes*, painful blisters that come and go
- *Hepatitis B*, perhaps the most highly contagious disease
- *Human papilloma virus (HPV)*, which produces genital warts
- *Human immunodeficiency virus (HIV)*, which destroys the body's ability to fight infections and leads to AIDS

History

STDs have been infecting people for thousands of years. In the 1400s, syphilis was so widespread that hundreds of people died from a syphilis plague that was called the "Great Pox."

The old diseases have not gone away, but modern medicine has found effective treatments for them. In the United States, the numbers of new cases of gonorrhea and syphilis have declined dramatically because antibiotics are readily available. Gonorrhea peaked in 1975 at a rate of 467.7 new reports for every 100,000 people; the rate dropped to 122.5 per

100,000 in 1997.[2] Syphilis was at its worse (since records began to be kept) in 1943, when 447 new cases were documented for every 100,000 people; in 1997, 17.5 cases per 100,000 were reported.[3]

While widespread use of antibiotics is causing the old STDs to wane, new diseases that do not respond to the same antibiotic treatments are spreading at alarming speeds. In 1993, chlamydia surpassed gonorrhea as the most common bacterial STD, with 179.5 cases per 100,000.[4] The numbers of people infected with herpes are steadily rising.

The incidence (occurrence) of sexually transmitted diseases has become so high that the Institute of Medicine has called it the "hidden epidemic"[5] because the diseases are spreading very rapidly, and little is being said or done about the problem. People who have STDs generally do not talk about them. Doctors do not routinely test for STDs or ask their patients about their sexual practices. Yet one American in five lives with an incurable STD, and millions more have sexually transmitted diseases that can be cured.[6]

Agents

The major STDs are caused by two types of microbes: bacteria and viruses. Gonorrhea, syphilis, and chlamydia are bacterial infections. Herpes, HPV/genital warts, hepatitis, and AIDS are viral.

Bacteria are microscopic, one-celled organisms. They thrive in moist, warm places and reproduce by dividing into two over and over again. They damage the tissues and the blood vessels at the site where they enter, and they continue their destruction as they multiply. The good news is that bacterial infections can be stopped with antibiotics. The bad news is that some strains of bacteria have mutated, or changed, so that they are resistant to the antibiotics that once eliminated them. Researchers are currently working to develop new, more powerful medicines.

Unlike bacteria, viruses cannot function on their own. These submicroscopic organisms are simply tiny, lifeless molecules of hereditary material, called DNA or RNA, surrounded by protective envelopes of protein. They can do nothing until they get inside a living organism. Once inside, the virus attaches to a host cell. Each type of virus chooses a specific host cell to attack. The virus, which cannot reproduce itself, fools the cell into copying the virus's DNA or RNA instead of its own. This activity destroys the host cell. As many as two hundred virus copies can be manufactured within a single host cell. The newly created viruses are released from the infected cell, find new host cells, and the process is repeated hundreds, then thousands, then millions of times.

The good news about viruses is that the body produces antibodies to fight the invaders, and when the body wins, the person is immune to that particular virus for life. The bad news is that the body does not always win. Viruses can hide in the body and cause repeat infections. No medicines have been found that can kill viruses, and for many people with a sexually transmitted viral disease, the virus is never completely gone.

In addition to bacteria and viruses, other organisms can cause STDs: protozoa, which are microscopic, single-cell animals (trichomoniasis); mites that burrow under the skin (scabies); and flat, wingless pubic lice (crabs).

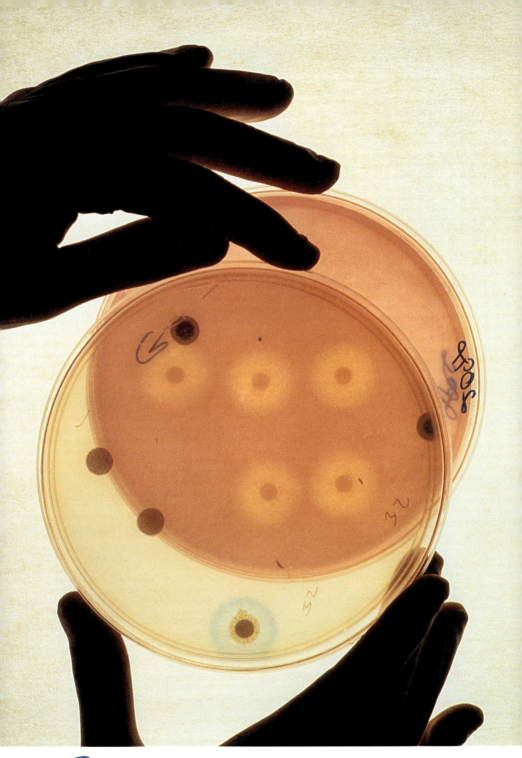

*B*acteria are microscopic organisms that can cause certain types of sexually transmitted diseases.

Transmission

The only way a person can get an STD is if the organism that causes the condition is passed from an infected person. Transmission occurs in one of three ways: (a) close sexual contact; (b) exchange of blood, usually through sharing of needles; and (c) passing of microbes before or during birth from an infected mother to a baby she is carrying.

Sexual contact. During any intimate sexual activity, an STD can be spread from one person to another. Microbes can move to or from the man's penis or the woman's vagina while the two are in direct contact during sexual intercourse, oral sex, or anal sex. As genital fluids pass from one body to another, infectious agents (organisms) are passed in those fluids. Germs that are in open sores in, on, or around the genitals or rectum can enter even microscopic cuts in a partner's body nearly any place that touches the sore. Transmission can occur even when the sex act is not completed.

STDs can also be transmitted by oral sex. If a person's lips or tongue come in contact with any infected fluid of a partner or with any sore caused by an STD, microbes enter the mouth. Some STDs that are spread this way leave sores in the mouth. It is possible, although very uncommon, for a person with an infected sore in the mouth to pass the disease by kissing.

It is also possible, although very unlikely, to become infected with STDs by handling an infected person's genitals. Infectious agents could enter the body through small cuts on the hands or fingers. Scabies and crabs are not always transmitted sexually; they can be picked up from infected clothing or bedding as well.

Exchange of blood. In addition to sexual activity, the sharing of needles has been a major factor in the spread of hepatitis and the AIDS virus (HIV). Because the diseases agents are in the blood, any activity during which the blood of an infected person can enter the body of another has the potential to transmit these diseases. Before 1985, when donated blood began to be carefully screened for AIDS, HIV (the virus that causes AIDS) was sometimes transmitted through blood transfusions.[7]

Mother to child. An infected mother can give an STD to a child she is carrying in her womb. Babies can be born with any sexually transmitted disease their mothers have.

Transmission myths. STDs are spread through sexual contact and contact with infected blood. They are *not* transmitted by casually touching people with the disease, by breathing the air they breathe, or by swimming in the same water with them. They are not passed by coughing or sneezing. They are

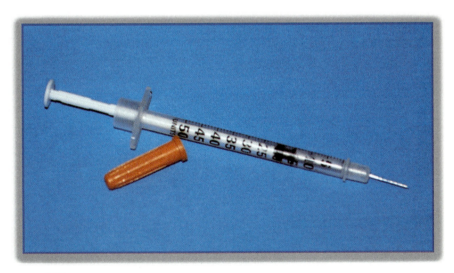

Sharing needles for illegal drug use can spread sexually transmitted diseases such as hepatitis and the AIDS virus.

Myths and Facts About STDs

Myth	People cannot get an STD the first time they have sex.
Fact	People can get an STD any time they have sex with an infected person.
Myth	A person can get AIDS by touching an infected person.
Fact	As with most STDs, AIDS is transmitted through sexual contact with an infected person or exposure to infected blood.
Myth	Only people who have sex a lot or with several different partners get STDs.
Fact	It takes only one sexual encounter with an infected person to get an STD.
Myth	People who use birth control pills are protected from STDs.
Fact	Birth control pills do not protect against STDs.
Myth	Washing or douching after intercourse protects against STDs.
Fact	Neither washing nor douching removes the microbes that cause STDs.
Myth	Having anal instead of vaginal intercourse protects against STDs.
Fact	Anal intercourse offers even more opportunities to contract STDs than vaginal intercourse.
Myth	Having oral instead of vaginal intercourse protects against STDs.
Fact	Many STDs can be transmitted through oral sex.
Myth	Using a condom correctly and consistently protects against all STDs.
Fact	Condoms do not always protect against herpes or HPV/genital warts.
Myth	A male cannot transmit an STD if he withdraws his penis before ejaculation.
Fact	STDs can be transmitted in pre-ejaculation fluid and from open sores.
Myth	A person with no visible signs of an STD does not need to be concerned.
Fact	Many people have no symptoms of some STDs for a long time. Everyone who is sexually active needs to be checked.
Myth	If doctors do not ask questions about sexual behavior, their patients probably do not have STDs.
Fact	Doctors do not always ask the right questions. Everyone who is sexually active, especially with more than one partner, needs to be checked.

not passed by touching things an infected person touches or by sitting on toilet seats they have used.

STDs can be caught during *any* sexual encounter. A person does not have to have sex many times in order to get an STD. One encounter is all it takes.

The pills, injections, and implants that protect against pregnancy have *no* effect on STDs. The jellies, foams, and creams that kill sperm do not protect against every STD. Washing or douching immediately after sex will not remove the microbes that cause the infections.

Some sexually transmitted diseases are easily cured, and others can be managed. But if left untreated, some can have devastating—even deadly—consequences.

Chapter 2

Paying the Piper: Consequences of STDs

She looked as if at any moment she might break into tears. She was slim, and wore blue jeans and a denim jacket.

"Twenty-two?"

"No, I'm nineteen."

"What's your complaint?"

"I don't know how to put it to you. You see, all my girlfriends made fun of me because I was still a virgin," she began, almost in a whisper. "So last Thursday, at a party, I let him do it," she finished with relief.

"So why did you do it . . . ?"

"Everybody made fun of me, and I really don't see any point in being a virgin. Besides, I had a couple of drinks."

"And now of course you are afraid you caught [a disease]?"

"Yes," she explained, "it hurts."[1]

Paying the Piper: Consequences of STDs

Ginny learned too late that her choices have consequences. Her decision to drink alcohol resulted in some loss of self-control. She chose to have sex and contracted an STD as a consequence. When having sex results in a disease, the cost of that choice can be very high. Depending on the specific infection and how soon it is diagnosed, the physical price might be minor discomfort, severe pain, or serious damage to the body. But the physical costs are only the beginning.

Irritation and Pain

The most common early signs indicating the presence of STDs are burning or pain during urination

Incubations for STDS	
Disease	**Time between infection and appearance of symptoms or antibodies**
Chancroid	4-10 days
Chlamydia	2 weeks for men, usually no symptoms for women
HPV/genital warts	3 weeks-9 months
Gonorrhea	1-30 days (average, 3-5 days)
Hepatitis	40-180 days (average 60-90 days)
Herpes	2-10 days
HIV/AIDS	3-6 months
Pubic lice (crabs)	5 days
Scabies	2-6 weeks
Syphilis	10-90 days
Trichomoniasis	2-28 days

Remember: For many people, some of these conditions have no symptoms.

Sexually Transmitted Diseases

and a discharge from the penis or vagina. Sometimes the sexual organs itch or burn; sometimes they swell. Sexually transmitted diseases can produce warts, bumps, blisters, rashes, and open sores. The sores are commonly in the genital area or around the rectum or the mouth. The first bumps and sores are sometimes very painful, sometimes merely irritating, and sometimes barely noticeable. They may itch or bleed. If the infection progresses unchecked, pain may be felt in the joints, muscles, abdomen, or back. One STD, pelvic inflammatory disease, causes sexual intercourse to be painful. Sexually transmitted diseases can cause a variety of problems throughout the body, including fever, nausea, and extreme tiredness.

The majority of people who get STDs do not know they have a disease for weeks and sometimes even months or years. Some diseases have no symptoms for a long time. Some people who have STDs never develop any symptoms.

Women are symptomless much more often than men. One reason a woman does not always experience immediate pain from an STD is that the germs frequently infect her cervix, which is located at the upper end of the vagina. The cervix has relatively few nerve fibers, so an infection on the cervix does not feel painful. Another reason is that the bumps and blisters that would be easy to see on a man's penis are often hidden inside a woman's body. Many females learn they have STDs only when they have a physical exam.

The absence of symptoms is not a good thing. When the infection is present, with or without physical indications, it can be passed to others. Some people are carriers: They carry the microbe and give it to others but never develop the condition themselves. Some diseases can appear to be gone for years and then break out again; they can be transmitted whether dormant or active. Perhaps the greatest problem with symptomless STDs is that, with some diseases, the undetected, untreated disease can, in time, do irreparable harm to the body.

Long-term Damage

The longer certain infectious organisms remain in the body, the greater damage they can cause. If ignored, some, such as chlamydia and gonorrhea, lead to sterility in both males and females. They can infect the sperm ducts in men and the fallopian tubes in women. As the sores heal, scar tissue is formed that blocks the passageways, making pregnancy impossible.

The consequences of some untreated STDs can extend far beyond the reproductive tract. The microbes can harm the joints, nerves, heart valves, blood vessels, spinal cord, and brain. Some STDs can produce arthritis, heart disease, paralysis, blindness, insanity, and death.

Having one STD increases a person's chances of contracting another, including HIV. Any disease weakens the body, making it easier prey for new infections. People with several sexual partners very often have more than one STD. HIV, the virus that causes AIDS, is particularly likely to occur in people with other sexually transmitted diseases because those infections frequently create breaks in the skin or the mucous membranes of the genital organs—breaks through which the virus can enter. Researchers have found that HIV transmission could

Symptoms and Possible STD and Non-STD Causes

Symptom	Possible STD	Possible Non-STD Cause
abdominal pain	PID, hepatitis, herpes	intestinal infection, inflamed appendix, ovulation, constipation
back pain	PID	muscle strain
bleeding from rectum	chancroid, trichomoniasis	
burning or pain during urination	chlamydia, herpes, trichomoniasis	urinary tract infection
discharge from penis or vagina	chlamydia, chancroid, herpes, gonorrhea, trichomoniasis	bladder infection, prostate infection, sexual arousal, yeast infection
fever	PID, hepatitis, herpes, AIDS	flu, cold, or other infection
genital itching or burning	gonorrhea, herpes, pubic lice, scabies	allergic reaction, yeast infection
nausea	PID, hepatitis, herpes	intestinal infection, pregnancy
pain during intercourse (females)	PID	
pain in muscles	herpes	strain or sprain
pain, swelling in joints	hepatitis, gonorrhea	arthritis, Lyme disease
rash	chlamydia, hepatitis, scabies, syphilis	allergic reaction, heat rash
sore throat	gonorrhea, syphilis	respiratory infection, strep throat, tonsillitis
sores, bumps, blisters	syphilis, chancroid, herpes, HPV, scabies	insect bite, infected pimple
swelling in lymph nodes	herpes, syphilis, HIV	any infection
swelling in genitals	chancroid, chlamydia, gonorrhea, trichomoniasis	
tiredness	hepatitis, AIDS	overactivity, lack of sleep
vaginal odor	trichomoniasis	yeast infection
yellowing skin and eyes	hepatitis	

be reduced by 42 percent or more if people with STDs were treated immediately.[2]

Emotional Costs

As destructive as the physical ravages of STDs can be, the psychological consequences are equally high. When people first learn they have an STD, they may experience a wide range of emotions: shock, embarrassment, self-pity, guilt, fear, or anger. Sometimes they feel betrayed. These infected people experience rejection and loneliness. For those in whom the disease has caused permanent damage, the prospect of cancer, disability, childlessness, or early death can be emotionally devastating.

Having an STD affects a person's relationship with his or her sexual partner. People may blame each other for bringing the disease into the relationship, and each may doubt the other's faithfulness. Since an STD can be present years before a diagnosis is made, its discovery might open up questions about past encounters that could be uncomfortable. Having to tell present and previous partners that they may have an STD is emotionally difficult. Some infections never go away completely, and recurrences can be unpleasant and painful.

Having an STD that never goes away impacts all future intimate relationships. With every new boyfriend or girlfriend, dozens of questions flood the mind. Will knowing an STD is present affect a new partner's opinion of the infected person? Who will want to be involved with someone who could transmit hepatitis, herpes, genital warts, or HIV? Will anyone choose to develop a deepening friendship with someone who is likely to die prematurely of AIDS? At what point in the relationship does someone

Sexually Transmitted Diseases

disclose this problem? How does a person bring up such a subject? What could happen if a couple wants to have children?

Costs to Babies

Some sexually transmitted diseases can be given by a mother to her baby during pregnancy or at the time of delivery. HIV can be transmitted after birth if a mother breastfeeds her infant.

During pregnancy, the bacteria or viruses that cause syphilis, hepatitis, or HIV enter the baby through blood shared with its mother. If the mother's syphilis, which is bacterial, is treated within the first three months of pregnancy, she will not pass the disease to her child. After the third month, however, an untreated mother has a greater than 70 percent chance of infecting her baby.[3] Syphilis transmitted to a baby while in the womb is called congenital syphilis. Its effects are serious: The bones and almost any organ of the baby's body can be severely damaged and misshapen, and as many as 40 percent of babies with syphilis die before birth.[4] Early examination of a pregnant woman can easily detect and prevent this tragedy, but because some expectant mothers do not get proper prenatal medical care, congenital syphilis still strikes newborns.

Unlike syphilis, the viral STDs hepatitis and HIV are more difficult to keep from a newborn. Seventy to 90 percent of all babies born to mothers with hepatitis are born with the virus. Fortunately, if these newborns are given a vaccine during their first day out of the womb, 90 to 95 percent will not develop full-blown hepatitis.[5]

For babies whose mothers have HIV, however, there is no vaccination. The use of antiviral drugs

Paying the Piper: Consequences of STDs

during pregnancy can sometimes keep HIV from reproducing in a newborn, but more than half of all infants born to infected mothers have the virus.[6]

Other STDs can affect a baby at birth if the disease-producing microbes are in the mother's vagina at the time of delivery. The effects on a newborn are considerably more serious than the symptoms in an adult. Chlamydia and gonorrhea can infect a baby's eyes, causing blindness. This is fairly rare now because most newborns are given

	Possible Consequences of Untreated STDs
Gonorrhea	inflammation of joints, arthritis, PID, sterility, increased risk of HIV/AIDS
Syphilis	blindness, paralysis, heart disease, mental illness, death, increased risk of HIV/AIDS
Chlamydia	inflammation of joints, arthritis, PID, sterility, increased risk of HIV/AIDS
PID	ectopic pregnancy, infertility, increased risk of HIV/AIDS
Herpes	miscarriage, premature birth, for babies: blindness, brain damage, death, increased risk of HIV/AIDS
Genital Warts	cancer of the cervix, increased risk of HIV/AIDS
Hepatitis	cirrhosis (scarring) of the liver, liver cancer, increased risk of HIV/AIDS
HIV/AIDS	death

Sexually Transmitted Diseases

antibiotic eyedrops to prevent this condition, which once afflicted as many as 15 percent of infants born in United States and European hospitals.[7] Chlamydia also causes infant pneumonia.

A mother with an active case of genital herpes can give the virus to her infant if the baby comes in

Some sexually transmitted diseases can be given by a mother to her baby, either during pregnancy or at the time of delivery.

contact with the sores during birth. Bumps and blisters can appear any place on the newborn's body, commonly on the sex organs and often on the vocal cords, making breathing difficult.

Even if they cause only minor discomfort to the mother, genital herpes can be extremely dangerous to a baby. If a mother has an outbreak at the time of delivery, especially a first outbreak, her baby can be born blind or brain damaged. Half of all infected newborns die, and half of the remainder have irreversible nerve damage.[8] However, herpes can be managed, and if no outbreak occurs at the time of delivery, a mother with the disease can usually have a healthy baby.

Because sexually transmitted diseases can be passed on to the next generation, the saying "Sex is for a moment but an STD is for a lifetime" is not absolutely true. An STD may be for two lifetimes, those of the mother and the newborn.

Chapter 3

The (SE)X Generation: Who Gets STDs?

Sylvia was sixteen years old. Her boyfriend, Ray, one year older, was the only person she had ever had intercourse with. Afterward she did not tell him about the feeling of pressure in her stomach or the burning sensation she felt. Then, she saw the small, red bumps near her vagina. Sylvia later discovered that she had herpes. How could she? They had only done it twice.[1]

Sara had bumps, too, and they would not go away. In fact, they got bigger, and more appeared each day. She finally went to a doctor, who told her they were genital warts. "I just lay there crying," she said. She did not consider herself promiscuous. She had had sex, but not with very many guys. "This shouldn't happen to me," she thought. "I'm a 'good girl.'"[2]

STDs *do* happen to "good girls"—and to "good boys," too. They happen to people who have had ten partners and to people who have had only one. They happen to people who have had sex fifty times and to those who have had sex just once. Only two kinds of people *cannot* contract a disease sexually: those who do not have sex and those who have sex only with one person who has not had an STD. Having only one sexual partner is called being monogamous. Two people who have intercourse only with each other are in a mutually monogamous relationship.

Although anyone who has sex outside a mutually monogamous relationship can get a disease, some people have a higher likelihood of being infected than others. Those at greatest risk are females and young people.

Females

Sexually transmitted diseases are a much bigger problem for women than for men. Generally, women get the diseases more easily, keep them longer, show symptoms less frequently, and have more serious consequences.

Women are more susceptible to STDs because their genitals have considerably more surface area than a man's penis, giving the microbes more opportunity to invade the body. In addition, during intercourse the fluids that might contain disease organisms are deposited directly into the woman's vagina, where infection can begin immediately. For a man, most of the woman's fluids surround rather than penetrate the penis, making it somewhat less likely for the germs to get in. In other words, it is much easier for a woman to get an STD from a man than for a man to get an STD from a woman. A woman is twice as likely as a man to contract a disease in a single encounter.[3]

When a woman acquires a sexually transmitted

infection, she often has no observable symptoms and so does not seek treatment. This permits the disease to spread and become more severe. Men, on the other hand, tend to experience symptoms much more quickly and may see a doctor sooner. So women remain infected longer than men—for example, almost three times as long with gonorrhea and chlamydia.[4]

Young People

Adolescents, especially teenage girls, have perhaps the greatest risk of acquiring STDs. Two thirds of the

Adolescents and STDs

- ✓ One fourth of all people with STDs are adolescents.
- ✓ Two thirds of all new STD cases are adolescents.
- ✓ Sexually active teens are three times more likely to have PID than women age twenty-five or older.
- ✓ One out of every four people newly infected with HIV is under age twenty-five.
- ✓ One third of all Americans with Hepatitis B are college-aged.
- ✓ 30 percent of all reported cases of syphilis occur in people under age twenty-five.
- ✓ 62 percent of all reported cases of gonorrhea occur in people under age twenty-five.
- ✓ 79 percent of women with chlamydia are age fifteen to twenty-four.
- ✓ One in four sexually active adolescent girls gets an STD every year.

The (SE)X Generation: Who Gets STDs?

STD cases diagnosed in the United States each year belong to people under the age of twenty-five.[5] Even for the diseases that are declining nationally, the rates among young people are rising. The rate of new syphilis infections in a five-year period among fifteen- to nineteen-year-old women jumped 130 percent in 1991 over the previous five-year period.[6] At the same time, one of every four new HIV infections was reported in people younger than twenty-two.[7] Pelvic inflammatory disease occurs three times as often in sexually active women under age twenty-five.[8] Every eleven seconds a teenager in the United States gets an STD.[9]

One of the reasons teenage girls get STDs so easily is that the adolescent cervix is still in a formative stage. The immature cells are easy targets for disease microbes. The main reasons, however, for the higher incidence of STDs generally and among teenagers more specifically are not physical but behavioral. In the last thirty years, people in the United States, and teenagers in particular, have been engaging in sex more often and with more partners.

More Sex, More Partners

Teenagers are beginning to explore sex at much younger ages than their parents did. Over one third of all adolescents in the United States have had intercourse before their fifteenth birthday,[10] and more than half have become sexually active by age seventeen.[11]

Once young people become sexually active, they usually continue to have sex, and they often move from one partner to another. Naturally, the more sexual partners a person has, the more that person may be exposed to a disease. In a sense, an individual

Sexually Transmitted Diseases

has sex with every person with whom his or her partner has had sex, because any untreated STD can continue to be transmitted to a chain of partners. The reason AIDS spread so quickly when it was first introduced into the United States is that those who contracted the disease had averaged sixty-one sex contacts during the year preceding diagnosis.[12]

Change in Attitudes About Sex

The increase in sexual activity and promiscuity (having several partners) among young people over the last three decades reflects an attitude of growing acceptance of teenage sex. Before the 1960s, most parents expected their children to refrain from sexual activity

*T*he increase in sexual activity among young people over the last three decades has led to an increase in cases of STDs.

until they married. Girls who got pregnant were looked down on. Parental and societal controls curbed much teenage sexual exploration.

In the 1960s, however, attitudes changed dramatically. Frustration and disillusionment surrounding the Vietnam War erupted in a rebellion against "the establishment"—the authority, the institutions, and the values of the older generation. Part of that rebellion was a sexual revolution. Young people of the sixties abandoned the restrictions of their elders in favor of "free love." In their push for liberation from the old attitudes, they rejected their parents' morality, giving up the association of right and wrong with specific sexual activities. Without moral limitations and free from social stigma, the new attitude was "Anything goes." What that meant, in practical terms, was more sex, beginning at younger ages, with more partners.

A number of developments that began in the 1960s made it possible for the free-love philosophy to become common practice. One was the increased availability and variety of birth control. With the introduction of the Pill, one reason for not having sex was removed. People no longer feared an unplanned pregnancy.

Another development was the radical restructuring of the traditional family. In 1960, 83 percent of children lived in families that included their biological fathers;[13] in the 1990s, more than half spend at least part of their childhood or youth in single-parent homes.[14] Coupled with an increase in the number of two-worker families, the revised family structure gives adolescents far less time under parental supervision and far more time with other teens. The primary influence on young people is no longer a set of parents, who might discourage premarital sex, but a group of peers, who are eager to explore their sexuality *now* rather than later.

Media

Perhaps as much as other teens, the media have had a profound impact on the sexual behavior of adolescents. The typical adolescent watches television twenty-two hours every week.[15] Add to that the time spent listening to the radio, and seven to nine hours a day are spent receiving messages from the electronic media[16]—more time than is spent on all other waking activities combined.

The content of that input is highly sexual. Each year, the average teenager in the United States sees almost fifteen thousand sexual incidents or allusions in television programs. In addition, teens view some twenty thousand commercials a year, many with the anything-but-subtle message that sex is a common, expected part of the adolescent experience.[17]

Not only television, but also films, videos, music, and magazines consumed by young people suggest that virginity is old-fashioned, multiple partners are fun, and frequent sex is the norm. At precisely the time in their lives when adolescents look outside their families to reaffirm or select the values that will determine their behavior, they are bombarded with images and sounds that say "Everyone is doing it."

But few of the movie characters get pregnant, much less contract a sexually transmitted disease. STDs do not make good song topics. The negative consequences of the behaviors portrayed in the media are rarely mentioned. Of the fifteen thousand sexual references teens view every year on television, barely one percent depict responsible sexual practices.[18] The behavior of teenagers mirrors the actions of their media idols, which are often irresponsible and full of risks.

Risky Behaviors

Taking risks is common in adolescence. Most young people rarely see beyond the present, so they have no fear of jeopardizing their future. They believe what psychologists call the invincibility myth: Nothing bad could possibly happen to them. Therefore, they cast off restraints, ignore warnings, and plunge headlong into what feels good at the moment.

Drinking alcohol can impair one's judgment and self-control, which can lead to risky sexual behavior. Such behavior puts a person at great risk for contracting an STD.

For many, sex feels good. Drinking and taking drugs, which lower the ability and desire to control oneself, feel good. And using protection feels bad. Even when they are aware of the potential consequences, adolescents tend to act not on what they know, but on what they feel. Therefore, many do not use condoms regularly. Knowledge does not always result in reduced risk.

Because more and more young people are engaging in these risky behaviors, today's teenagers suffer more from sexually transmitted diseases than any other generation in history.

Chapter 4

Types of Infection: The Diseases

Summer vacation at the beach was great fun for fifteen-year-old Greg. He and his friends especially enjoyed cruising on the boardwalk. On one of those cruises, they met some girls and the partying that followed included sex. That was the first and only time Greg ever saw those girls.

But ten days later, Greg's hips started to ache. When his penis began itching the next day, he noticed a small cluster of blisters on it. Greg showed his father, and his father took him to a doctor. Greg had genital herpes.

The cream the doctor gave Greg took away most of the pain, but a month later it was back again. So, in addition to the cream, Greg had to take some expensive pills to keep the infection from recurring so often. He will probably have to take them for the rest of his life.[1]

Greg was fortunate. He consulted a doctor who was able to treat him. Other people may not be as lucky. They may put off seeking medical attention, or their doctors may not ask the right questions. It is wise for everyone, especially those who are sexually active, to know the signs and symptoms of the most common STDs.

Gonorrhea

Gonorrhea begins as an infection in the genitals, the rectum, or the throat. Once in the body, the bacteria can travel in the bloodstream to the knees, elbows, fingers, or other joints, where they cause painful inflammation and acute arthritis. Microbes can also be carried by the blood to the skin, where pus-filled pimples break out between the fingers or on the arms or legs. Scarring can block male sperm ducts and female fallopian tubes, resulting in sterility. In women, the infection can eventually produce pelvic inflammatory disease.

About 80 percent of infected women and 20 to 25 percent of infected men have no symptoms until the disease has spread far beyond the initial infection. Others notice a burning sensation and a discharge, usually three to five days after contracting the infection. This discharge has given rise to the nicknames "drip" and "morning drop." Gonorrhea is also called "the clap." The disease is highly contagious very soon after a person gets it, even before any symptoms appear.

Since the development of antibiotics, gonorrhea has become curable. New strains of bacteria have developed that do not respond to the antibiotics penicillin or tetracycline, so gonorrhea is now treated with ceftriaxone.

Syphilis

Like gonorrhea, syphilis starts as a simple infection that is easily unnoticed. But it can do more damage to the body than any other bacterial STD. In the first, or primary, stage, the microbes dig their way underneath the skin of the penis or the vagina. There they reproduce, erupting through the skin in a chancre, a painless sore. The chancre heals in one to six weeks, but the infection spreads throughout the body via the blood.

One to six months later, the secondary stage begins. A skin rash appears almost anywhere and sometimes everywhere, often accompanied by fever and headache. Like the chancres, the rash disappears on its own after two to six weeks, but the infection remains.

Often the disease goes into a latent (quiet) period during which nothing seems wrong. This period can

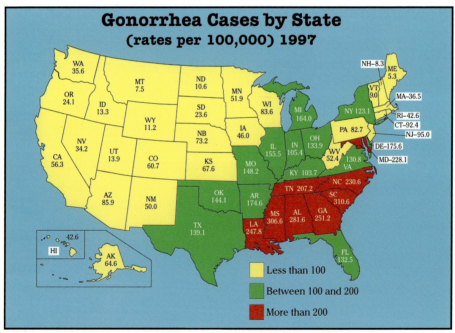

Source: U.S. Department of Health and Human Services, Public Health Service, Centers for Disease Control and Prevention (CDC), *STD Surveillance 1997*, September 1998.

The total rate of gonorrhea for the United States in 1997 was 120.9 cases per 100,000 people.

last for months or even many years. During that time, the bacteria are destroying cells in the nerves, spine, liver, kidneys, bones, heart, or brain. The obvious and severe damage to these parts of the body mark the third and final stage. About one third of all people with syphilis progress to the third stage because the infection is difficult to detect. The sores do not hurt and often are not seen. The rash is sometimes so mild it is ignored. But when found, syphilis is easily cured if treated before the third stage. It has not yet developed a resistance to penicillin.

Chlamydia

The most common STD in the United States today, more widespread than all the others put together, is chlamydia. The symptoms and effects are much like those of gonorrhea, but chlamydia is even more difficult to detect. The chlamydia bacteria take longer to reproduce, so symptoms do not appear for at least two weeks and the infection usually spreads farther before any problem is suspected. Most women and a quarter of all men have no initial signs.

Women get chlamydia six times more often than men, predominantly young women. Thirty-three percent of all infected females are between twenty and twenty-four years of age, and 46 percent are from fifteen to nineteen years old.[2] The infection poses a much greater threat to women because it can travel up the reproductive tract and produce pelvic inflammatory disease.

Pelvic Inflammatory Disease

Pelvic inflammatory disease (PID) is not transmitted sexually but is a secondary infection that often follows untreated gonorrhea or chlamydia. It is an

Sexually Transmitted Diseases

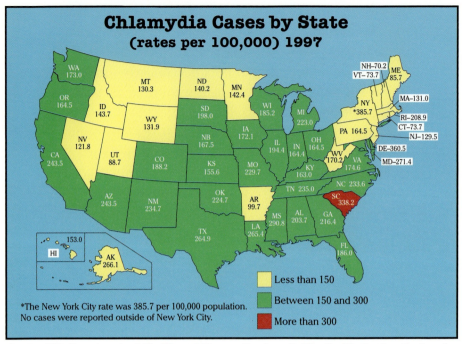

Source: U.S. Department of Health and Human Services, Public Health Service, Centers for Disease Control and Prevention (CDC), *STD Surveillance 1997*, September 1998.

*T*he total rate of chlamydia for the United States in 1997 was 204.7 cases per 100,000 people.

inflammation of the uterus, the fallopian tubes, or both. The first sign of PID is usually abdominal pain, frequently quite severe. Other symptoms include abnormal bleeding, fever, nausea, and backache. Intercourse may be painful.

As a woman's body fights the infection in her fallopian tubes, scars form on the inside walls, blocking eggs from traveling down the tubes to the uterus. In 20 percent of women with PID, blocked tubes cause permanent infertility, the inability to ever have children.[3] In others, an egg may get far enough to be fertilized by a sperm cell but is unable to travel the rest of the way to the uterus. This is called an ectopic pregnancy—a pregnancy in the wrong place. Ectopic pregnancies are very dangerous, even life-threatening.

The permanent damage cannot be reversed, but pelvic inflammatory disease can be cured. Because PID is generally severe by the time it is detected, treatment must begin immediately, before time-consuming tests can reveal which microbes are responsible. Women are usually given a number of medications at the same time to kill all possible disease agents. Since gonorrhea and chlamydia are so prevalent, however, recurrences of PID are common. Each repeat bout with the disease is usually more severe and more dangerous than the preceding one.

Herpes

The herpes simplex virus (HSV) is not carried in blood; it is found on and directly under the skin of infected people. Therefore, it does not invade the body through cuts or other openings, but through the skin. The virus comes in two forms. HSV1, which can be transmitted sexually or nonsexually, causes sores that usually appear in and around the mouth. HSV2 produces sores primarily in the genital region.

Sores from either strain can appear wherever the virus enters the body: on or around the penis, vagina, anus, mouth, buttocks, thighs, or fingers. Herpes sores look at first like small, red pimples. They itch for a few hours, then ache and burn. After about a day, they look like clusters of blisters, which break open. The painful sores heal in two to three weeks.

But the virus is not gone. It hides in nerve cells beneath the skin. Then weeks, months, or years later, the virus travels up the nerve fiber and erupts again at the same spots as the first time. Some people break out frequently, every week or two; others may have only one or two recurrences ever. The average is four incidents a year.[4] Repeat outbreaks are usually milder and do not last as long as the first. Even before the bumps appear, the virus is present on the skin's surface and the disease is contagious. About two thirds of infected people do not notice any symptoms but can still pass the infection to a partner.

Genital Warts

Genital warts are caused by the human papilloma virus (HPV). HPV stays in the cells just under the skin and can grow new warts at any time—weeks,

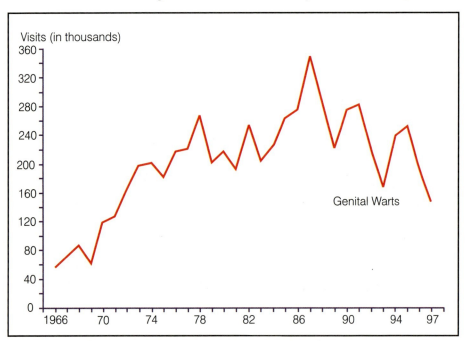

Source: National Disease and Therapeutic Index (IMS America, Ltd.)

This graph shows the initial visits to physicians' offices by people suffering from genital warts.

months, or even years later. Because the warts take a long time to develop, usually about three months, and may not appear at all in some people who carry the virus, this STD is very common.

The warts appear at the spots where the microbe entered the body—on the penis, inside or outside the vagina, around the anus, or sometimes around the mouth. They are transmitted not through fluids, not through openings in the skin, but through skin-to-skin contact. Because they do not travel to other sites, they are passed almost exclusively through sexual activity. They can be hidden inside the vagina and can be painless, so people might not realize they have the disease. But with or without noticeable symptoms, they are highly contagious.

The warts are easy to distinguish from the eruptions of herpes. They usually look like tiny cauliflowers, little lumps one quarter of an inch across and three eighths of an inch high.[5] They do not break open, and they do not always go away by themselves. They can be removed with creams or gels, frozen off chemically, burned away with an electric needle, vaporized by a laser beam, or cut out surgically. But the virus remains. It lives in cells just below the skin's surface.

Genital warts may appear to be little more than nuisances, but the infection is, in fact, extremely serious. Of the seventy known strains of HPV, at least ten are thought to produce cancer of the cervix in women. HPV is probably responsible for 80 percent of all cases of cervical cancer, an affliction that kills four thousand nine hundred women each year.[6] The two strains that are associated with visible warts usually do not lead to cancer.

Sexually Transmitted Diseases

Hepatitis

At least five different hepatitis virus strains, A through E, attack the liver, sometimes resulting in cirrhosis (hardening) of the liver. Hepatitis B, the most serious, can be transmitted sexually.

The hepatitis B virus, one hundred times more contagious than HIV,[7] is carried in the blood and in other body fluids, including genital fluids, saliva, perspiration, and tears. It can live for as long as one week outside the body, so it can be transmitted on objects such as toothbrushes, earrings, nail files, and razors.[8] Half the people who have the virus develop no symptoms. Those who do have symptoms may think they have the flu; they suffer fever, nausea, fatigue, diarrhea, and achiness. The disease is well advanced before the telltale yellowing of skin and eyes is evident.

For awhile, most people with hepatitis B were homosexual men, people who injected drugs, or health care workers who were exposed to infected blood. In the 1980s, however, the disease began to spread rapidly because of the hardiness of the hepatitis virus and the fact that it can be passed indirectly, on items tainted by infected blood. The disease is especially widespread among adolescents because of their multiple sexual partners. More than one third of the three hundred thousand people infected each year are college-aged.[9]

Although no cure for hepatitis has yet been found, a vaccine, available since 1985, is 90 percent effective at preventing the disease.[10]

HIV/AIDS

Probably the most feared of all sexually transmitted diseases is AIDS—with good reason. Although

Types of Infection: The Diseases

medications are being developed in attempts to cure or prevent HIV infection, at present, AIDS is always fatal. More than 380,000 of the 640,993 Americans reported to be infected from 1981 to 1997 have already died—nearly 60 percent.[11] At least another million Americans have the human immunodeficiency virus (HIV), which eventually develops into AIDS.[12] In 1992, only eleven years after the first case of AIDS was diagnosed in the United States, HIV infection became the leading cause of death among young men and the third leading killer of young women. The Centers for Disease Control project that, by the year 2000, HIV will be the number one cause of death among all Americans.[13]

The acronym "AIDS" stands for Acquired Immunodeficiency Syndrome. "Acquired" means that the condition is not inherited; it comes from infection with HIV. "Immunodeficiency" indicates that the disease renders the immune system deficient; it destroys the cells that fight infection. AIDS is a "syndrome," which means that a group of conditions defines the disease; different individuals may display different symptoms. People are diagnosed as having AIDS when they have HIV infection and one or more of twenty-five specific, serious medical conditions such as fever or diarrhea lasting more than a month, weight loss without dieting, extreme tiredness, or loss of a sense of balance.[14]

HIV, the virus that causes AIDS, is found in blood and other body fluids. It is transmitted primarily through sharing needles while injecting drugs (25 percent) and sexual activity (66 percent).[15] It can also be passed from mother to child before or during birth and during breastfeeding. The presence of any other STD raises a person's susceptibility to HIV infection because any disease weakens the body's ability to fight another and because open sores are doorways to the bloodstream.

The cells the virus uses to reproduce itself are the cells of the immune system, and viruses destroy the cells they use. So an HIV infection can do a great deal of damage long before it reaches the AIDS stage. Any infection to which an infected person is exposed is dangerous because HIV erodes the body's self-defenses. People with HIV infection are particularly susceptible to Kaposi's sarcoma, a rare skin cancer, and a type of pneumonia known as PCP, both of which are usually fatal. But any disease, no matter how mild, can be devastating to someone with HIV infection.

Within the first month after the HIV infection occurs, at least half of all infected people feel ill. They have fever, aches, fatigue, sore throat, and swollen lymph glands.[16] But such ailments are easily dismissed, especially when they disappear fairly quickly. Usually no new symptoms appear until years later, when some minor infection cannot be shaken. During the intervening time, when all seems well, the virus is easily passed to others.

As with all viral STDs, no cure has been found for AIDS. A regimen of drugs, however, has been developed that slows the course of the virus and actually reduces HIV levels in the blood. The regimen is a combination of protease inhibitors, which slow down the virus's attack on the immune system, and antiviral medications, which keep the virus from reproducing. The treatment is often referred to as a drug cocktail because it is a mixture of medicines.

Chapter 5

After the Party: What Should People With STDs Do?

Carol did not want to have sex, but her boyfriend forced himself upon her. She decided that she would not go out with him any more. She never wanted to see him again.

But he had left her a reminder of their night together. She did not know the bumps meant she had genital herpes, but she knew something was wrong. She knew she should go to a doctor, but she did not want her parents to find out. So she did nothing for six months—nothing except cry. Finally she mustered enough courage to talk with a girlfriend. That friend took Carol to a clinic where she got free treatment with no questions asked. Her disease is not cured—it will be with her for life—but the medication relieves some of the pain and shortens the duration of each outbreak. It is still bothersome, but it is manageable.[1]

▼ ▼ ▼

Having a sexually transmitted disease is a painful, frightening, and dangerous experience, but it is not the end of the world. Nonviral STDs can be cured, and viral STDs can be controlled to some extent. Dealing with an STD involves three steps: testing, treatment, and telling any partners.

Testing

Anyone who is sexually active outside a mutually monogamous relationship should be tested periodically for STDs. Many people, especially women, experience no symptoms from some diseases for a long time, but they could very well be infected and be passing the microbes on to others. At the same time, the disease could be silently damaging their bodies. So, whether they suspect an STD or not, sexually active people should ask their doctors to test them.

For someone who does not have or is not able to go to a doctor, public health clinics are almost always available to detect and treat STDs, usually at no charge. They can be located by looking in a telephone book under the state, county, or city department of health. Other agencies sometimes offer free testing and treatment; they can be found by calling one of the hotlines listed at the end of this book. (In most states, laws allow doctors to treat minors for STDs without parental consent.)

Different tests are needed to identify different diseases. For infections that produce discharges and those that have open sores, the discharge or the scrapings from the blisters are examined under powerful microscopes. HPV is positively identified through microscopic examination of tissue from genital warts. More thorough but more time-consuming tests usually follow, allowing precise identification of the infectious agent. Knowing which disease is present is important because each infection responds to a specific medication.

After the Party: What Should People With STDs Do?

The STDs in which the microbes are carried in the blood are detected through blood analysis. Separate tests are conducted to determine the presence of HIV, hepatitis, and syphilis. Some of the procedures work by looking for antibodies the body has produced in response to the infection, and it may take as long as six months or more for those antibodies to be developed. The disease may be raging long before antibodies are present. Therefore, blood tests with negative results are usually repeated in six months.

Treatment

Once a sexually transmitted disease is diagnosed, treatment should begin promptly. Bacterial STDs respond well to antibiotics. Each disease is treated by a specific medication for a specific length of time. Pelvic inflammatory disease, because it can result from one or more of any number of infectious agents, is generally treated with multiple drugs.[2] If treatment is begun early enough, any bacterial STD can be cured.

The treatment regimen must be followed exactly as prescribed. Symptoms often disappear and people feel better after just a few doses of antibiotics, but if all the medication is not taken, all the microbes are probably not destroyed, and the disease will erupt again. At the end of the treatment program, a retest is given to confirm that no bacteria remain. Sexual activity must be halted until the treatment has ended and the disease is gone. Otherwise, a person under treatment can still give the infection to someone else and can become infected again with the same or another STD. Antibiotics do not give immunity against new infections.

Sexually Transmitted Diseases

*A*lthough antibiotics can cure bacterial sexually transmitted diseases, they do not effect viral STDs at all.

Antibiotics do not affect viral STDs; no cure has yet been found for viruses. Antiviral medications can slow the advance of the viruses and thus keep the diseases somewhat under control. For viral STDs, treatment is focused on symptoms: Genital warts can be removed, and the pain often associated with herpes outbreaks can be soothed with aspirin or other pain relievers. So far, no effective treatment has been found for hepatitis. Some experimental drugs may help, but their success is only slight, and they are very expensive and have unpleasant side effects. One—alpha interferon—costs about three hundred dollars a week and must be taken for four to six months. Even a liver transplant, which replaces the organ the virus attacks, is seldom done because the virus hides in other organs, emerging to infect the new liver.[3]

As with hepatitis, no cure has been found for HIV. The infections that AIDS patients suffer because of their weakened immune systems can be treated. But no one yet has succeeded in destroying or removing the HIV virus. Some antiviral medications protect cells against invasion by the virus; others keep infected cells from producing new virus organisms.[4] A combination of three different types of drugs is beginning to be remarkably effective at slowing the progression of HIV infection. Researchers hope that this "triple-therapy cocktail" will soon enable them to control the disease.[5]

Treatment for STDs

Disease	Treatment	Type of Treatment	Effect
gonorrhea	1. penicillin or tetracycline 2. ceftriaxone or cefixime	1. antibiotic 2. antibiotic	many strains are resistant cure
syphilis	penicillin	antibiotic	cure
chlamydia	oloxacin, azithromycin, tetracycline, or doxycycline	antibiotic	cure
PID	several antibiotics at the same time	antibiotic	cure
herpes	acyclovir	antiviral	relieve pain and reduce length of outbreak
genital warts	1. podophyllin or pedofilox 2. liquid nitrogen 3. electric needle 4. CO_2 laser 5. cutting	1. chemical 2. freezing 3. burning 4. laser 5. surgery	all treatments remove present warts
hepatitis	alpha interferon	antiviral	25% effective in reducing progression
HIV/AIDS	"cocktail" of indinavir, zidovudine, and laminudine	antiviral	slows progression and may reduce levels of HIV

Partner Notification

Just as soon as a positive diagnosis has been made, people with STDs need to notify everyone from whom they may have gotten the disease and to whom they may have given it. Partner notification is essential for stopping the infections from spreading to new people and preventing reinfection. Prompt notification may also keep another person from experiencing serious complications from untreated diseases.

Some STDs have a long incubation—the period of time between when the infectious agent enters the body and when symptoms begin to appear. The hepatitis, HPV, and HIV viruses can each be in the body for six months or longer before they are detected. Because of the variety of incubations, anyone who has had sex with an infected person within twelve months prior to discovery of the disease should be told.

The thought of telling a partner may be uncomfortable, but the act itself is really not difficult. All that needs to be said is, "I have found out I have a sexually transmitted disease. You may have it too, so you need to be checked." For some partners, the first reaction will be anger, but the anger will probably not last as long as the consequences of an untreated STD. Telling a partner is the caring thing to do and the responsible thing to do.

Taking charge of one's own body—making the choices and carrying through with the actions that prevent STDs—is another caring and responsible thing to do.

Chapter 6

Taking Charge: How to Prevent STDs

Frank was slouched in his seat, arms folded, head slung back, chin held high. The sex-ed teacher was on her soapbox again, drilling the class on the benefits of the condom. Next to abstinence, she was saying, the condom is the most effective protection against pregnancy and disease. Frank just laughed. At fifteen, he knew all he needed to know about sex. He knew how it worked and how he liked it. When the teacher tried to push him to admit that using a condom was a loving act, he sneered defiantly, "I don't use a condom for anybody!"

But before the school year was over, Frank's defiance was gone. He was one of the few males who do not feel the early symptoms of gonorrhea. By the time he finally saw a physician, the doctor was not sure if the infection had permanently blocked Frank's sperm duct. If it had, then Frank would never have children.[1]

Frank's disease, and every other nonviral STD, is curable when detected early. All STDs are completely preventable. The epidemic can be stopped in

Sexually Transmitted Diseases

an individual and in a community when those who are most vulnerable take charge of their own sexual practices.

Eliminate Risky Behaviors

The first step in taking charge is to refuse to participate in the activities that place people at the highest risk of contracting STDs. This means, for one thing, not drinking or taking drugs. Apart from the danger of blood contact with injectable drugs, alcohol and drugs cloud judgment. In a 1997 nationwide survey of 720 girls, 85 percent said that drinking was a major factor leading to sex.[2]

Another high-risk practice is anal sex. Diseases are spread more easily during anal intercourse because the blood vessels lining the rectum break easily, creating more openings for infections to enter and releasing blood that might pass infections to another person. Germs deposited in the rectum have a direct route to the bloodstream, and germs already in the rectum can easily surround and infect a partner's penis.[3]

Having multiple partners places many young people at great risk for STDs. Each partner brings to the sexual

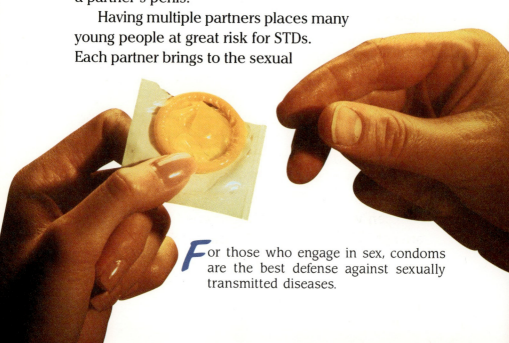

*F*or those who engage in sex, condoms are the best defense against sexually transmitted diseases.

encounter all the germs accumulated from all earlier sexual activity with all previous partners.

Choose a Partner Carefully

Taking charge means choosing when and with whom to have sex rather than just letting things happen. More than 80 percent of adolescent girls have sex because boys pressure them or because they are afraid they will lose a boyfriend if they do not.[4] Since the consequences of having sex can be enormous, serious thought should be given to selecting a partner. Someone with obvious sores or rashes in the genital area would not be a wise choice. Neither is an individual who is known to go from partner to partner. The safest partner is one who has never had sex or who has been tested and is disease-free. Remaining with that partner only, in a monogamous relationship, ensures protection from STDs.

Condoms

For those who choose to engage in sex, the best defense against sexually transmitted disease is the latex condom. The thin sheath placed over the penis during intercourse prevents the exchange of bodily fluids and any microbes that might be lurking in those fluids.

For adequate protection, the condom must be used any and every time people have sex. And it must be used correctly. It must be put on before the penis is inserted into the partner's body and held in place while the still-erect penis is withdrawn.

Even with consistent and correct use, condoms are not 100 percent effective against STDs. They can break, slip partially or completely off, or be scratched by fingernails. A female condom is subject to some

Using a Condom

1. Use a new, *latex* condom for each act of intercourse.
2. Put the condom on as soon as the penis is erect, *before any sexual contact.*
3. *Pinch the tip* of the condom and unroll it onto the erect penis. Pinching the tip makes a little pouch that collects fluids and keeps the condom from breaking.
4. *Lubricate* the condom with a water-based lubricant, *not* petroleum jelly, lotion, or baby oil because these can weaken the condom. A nonoxynol-9 lubricant can kill some STD microbes.
5. Withdraw immediately after having sex, before the penis goes soft. *Hold the condom firmly* to keep it from slipping off.

of the same possibilities. Furthermore, condoms do not protect against the very common diseases that are transmitted through skin-to-skin contact rather than through bodily fluids—herpes and genital warts. The contagious sores and warts are often located on areas not covered by the latex condom.

Abstinence

Only one behavior is a foolproof, absolute guarantee against sexual transmission of disease: abstaining from sex. A person who chooses to refrain from sexual activity is spared the irritation of a painful infection and the worry about long-term physical damage. Abstinence removes the fear of exposure to an incurable disease and eliminates the emotional turmoil of sexually troubled relationships.

Whether a person has never had sex or has had sex one hundred times with one hundred different people . . . whether someone has been treated and is currently free of an STD or has a virus that will probably never go away . . . it is never too late to take charge of one's sexual life. Whatever is a product of the past can be treated or managed. What happens in the future depends on today's choices. From this point on, for every new opportunity for contracting a sexually transmitted disease, every STD can be prevented.

Where to Find Help

HOTLINES

800 numbers are free; others may cost.

Automated information on hepatitis
404-332-4555

American Liver Foundation
Information on hepatitis: 800-223-0179

National Herpes Hotline
919-361-8488

National HIV/AIDS Hotline
800-342-AIDS;
(800-342-2437);
Spanish: 800-344-SIDA;
(800-344-7432);
Hearing impaired: 800-243-7889

National STD Hotline
800-227-8922

WEB SITES

Centers for Disease Control and Prevention
<http://www.cdc.gov>

HIV prevention fact sheets in English and Spanish from University of California/ San Francisco Center for AIDS Prevention
<http://www.caps.ucsf.edu/FSindex.html>

Introduction

1. Patricia Hittner, "Deadly Denial: How Our Daughters Risk Everything," *Better Homes and Gardens*, October 1994, pp. 54–59.

Chapter 1. Hidden Epidemic: What STDs Are All About

1. Eddie C. Sollie, *Straight Talk with Your Gynecologist: How to Get Answers That Will Save Your Life* (Hillsboro, Oreg.: Beyond Words, 1992), p. 18.

2. U.S. Department of Health and Human Services, Public Health Service, Centers for Disease Control and Prevention (CDC), *Sexually Transmitted Disease Surveillance 1997*, September 1998, pp. 65–66.

3. Ibid.

4. Ibid.

5. S. Sternberg, "Risky Sex Breeds Neglected Epidemic," *Science News*, 150, vol. 22, November 30, 1996, p. 343.

6. John Sedgwick, "Beware of STDs," *Self*, July 1995, p. 518.

7. U.S. Department of Health and Human Services, Public Health Service, Centers for Disease Control and Prevention (CDC), *Fact Sheet: AIDS*, n.d.

Chapter 2. Paying the Piper: Consequences of STDs

1. Basile Yanovsky, *The Dark Fields of Venus: From a Doctor's Logbook* (New York: Harcourt Brace Jovanovich, 1973), pp. 36–37.

2. Marie Laga, "STD Control for HIV Prevention—It Works!," *Lancet*, 346, August 26, 1995, p. 518.

3. U.S. Department of Health and Human Services, Public Health Service, Centers for Disease Control and Prevention (CDC), *Sexually Transmitted Disease Surveillance 1995*, September 1996, p. 19.

4. Ibid.

5. Beth Livermore, "The Stealth STD," *Glamour*, August 1994, p. 46.

6. G. B. Scott et al., "Mothers of Infants with Acquired Immunodeficiency Syndrome: Evidence of Both Symptomatic and Asymptomatic Carriers," *Journal of the American Medical Association*, 253, 1985, pp. 363–366.

7. King K. Holmes, Per-Anders Mårdh, P. Frederick Sparling, Paul J. Wiesner, Willard Cates, Jr., Stanley M. Lemon, Walter E. Stamm, eds., *STDs*, 2nd ed. (New York: McGraw-Hill, 1990), p. 804.

8. Patricia Hittner, "Deadly Denial: How Our Daughters Risk Everything," *Better Homes and Gardens*, October 1994, p. 56.

Chapter 3. The (SE)X Generation: Who Gets STDs?

1. Personal interview, August 1997.

2. Lauren Picker, "Prevent Sexually Transmitted Diseases," *American Health*, 14, vol. 8, October 1995, p. 62.

3. Hilary Hinds Kitasei, "STDs: What You Don't Know Can Hurt You," *Ms.,* vol. 5, March–April 1995, p. 24.

4. Ibid.

5. U.S. Department of Health and Human Services, Public Health Service, Centers for Disease Control and Prevention (CDC), Division of STD/HIV Prevention, *Annual Report*, 1990.

6. Ruth Mayer, "Sex Plagues of the '90s," *Mademoiselle*, January 1994, p. 111.

7. Philip S. Rosenberg, Robert J. Biggar, and James J. Goedert, "Declining Age at HIV Infection in the United States," *New England Journal of Medicine*, 330, March 17, 1994, p. 789.

8. William M. McCormack, "Pelvic Inflammatory Disease," *New England Journal of Medicine*, 330, January 13, 1994, pp. 115–117.

9. U.S. Department of Health and Human Services, Public Health Service, Centers for Disease Control and Prevention (CDC), *AIDS Prevention Guide*, n.d.

10. Peggy Clarke, "Teen-Age Sex Survey Would Teach Risks," *The New York Times*, August 7, 1991.

11. Carnegie Council on Adolescent Development, *Great Transitions: Preparing Adolescents for a New Century* (New York: Carnegie Corporation of New York, 1995), p. 40.

12. Lyn R. Frumkin and John M. Leonard, *Questions and Answers on AIDS* (Los Angeles: Health Information Press, 1997), p. 69.

13. David Popenoe, "Where's Papa?" *Utne Reader*, September–October 1996, p. 68. (Excerpted from *Life Without Father*, [Free Press, 1996].)

14. D. Hernandez, *America's Children: Resources from Family, Government, and the Economy* (New York: Russell Sage Foundation, 1993).

15. V. C. Strasburger, *Adolescents and the Media: Medical and Psychological Impact* (Newbury Park, Calif.: Sage, 1995), cited in Carnegie Council on Adolescent Development, p. 115.

16. Dianne Hales, "How Teenagers See Things," *Parade Magazine*, August 18, 1996, p. 5. National survey of adolescents conducted for the Horatio Alger Association.

17. Victor C. Strasburger, "Tuning in to Teenagers, *Newsweek*, May 19, 1997.

18. Ibid.

Chapter 4. Types of Infection: The Diseases

1. Alan E. Nourse, *Teen Guide to Safe Sex* (New York: Franklin Watts, 1988), p. 8.

2. "Chlamydia Trachomatis Genital Infections—United States, 1995," *Journal of the American Medical Association*, 277, March 26, 1997, pp. 952–953.

3. U.S. Department of Health and Human Services, Public Health Service, Centers for Disease Control and Prevention (CDC), *Sexually Transmitted Disease Surveillance 1997*, September 1998, p. 37.

4. U.S. Department of Health and Human Services, Public Health Service, Centers for Disease Control and Prevention (CDC), *Fact Sheet: Herpes*, n.d.

5. U.S. Department of Health and Human Services, Public Health Service, Centers for Disease Control and Prevention (CDC), *Fact Sheet: Genital Warts*, n.d.

6. S. Sternberg, "Risky Sex Breeds Neglected Epidemic," *Science News*, 150, vol. 22, November 30, 1996, p. 343.

7. "Students at Risk from Hepatitis B," *U.S.A. Today*, 122, January 1994, p. 8.

8. Beth Livermore, "The Stealth STD," *Glamour*, August 1994, p. 46.

9. "Students at Risk," p. 8.

10. Livermore, p. 46.
11. U.S. Department of Health and Human Services, Public Health Service, Centers for Disease Control and Prevention (CDC), *HIV/AIDS Surveillance Report*, vol. 9, No. 2, December 1997, p. 19.
12. U.S. Department of Health and Human Services, Public Health Service, Centers for Disease Control and Prevention (CDC), *Fact Sheet: AIDS*, n.d.
13. Lyn R. Frumkin and John M. Leonard, *Questions and Answers on AIDS* (Los Angeles: Health Information Press, 1997), pp. 127–128.
14. Ibid., pp. 17–18.
15. Ibid., p. 56.
16. Ibid., p. 28.

Chapter 5. After the Party: What Should People With STDs Do?

1. Personal interview, Fall 1997.
2. William M. McCormack, "Pelvic Inflammatory Disease," *New England Journal of Medicine*, 330, January 13, 1994, pp. 115–117.
3. Beth Livermore, "The Stealth STD," *Glamour*, August 1994, pp. 46–49.
4. Paul Harding Douglas and Laura Pinsky, *The Essential AIDS Fact Book* (New York: Pocket Books, 1996), p. 66.
5. Scott M. Hammer et al., "A Controlled Trial of Two Nucleoside Analogues Plus Indinavir in Persons with Human Immunodeficiency Virus Infection and CD4 Cell Counts of 200 per Cubic Millimeter or Less," *New England Journal of Medicine*, 337, September 11, 1997, pp. 725–731; Roy M. Gulick et al., "Treatment with Indinavir and Lamivudine in Adults with Human Immunodeficiency Virus Infection and Prior Antiretroviral Therapy," *New England Journal of Medicine*, 337, September 11, 1997, pp. 734–737.

Chapter 6. Taking Charge: How to Prevent STDs

1. Personal interview, Summer 1997.
2. Sey Chessler, "What Teenage Girls Say About Pregnancy," *Parade Magazine*, February 2, 1997, p. 4.
3. Eddie C. Sollie, *Straight Talk with Your Gynecologist: How to Get Answers That Will Save Your Life* (Hillsboro, Oreg.: Beyond Words, 1992), p. 211.
4. Chessler, p. 4.

abstinence—Choosing not to have sex.

acquired immunodeficiency syndrome (AIDS)—STD that is the last stage of HIV infection, an infection of the immune system.

agent—Bacteria, virus, or other microbe that causes a disease.

antibiotic—Medicine that kills bacteria.

antibody—Substance produced by the immune system to fight off invaders such as viruses.

bacteria—Single-celled, microscopic plants.

cervix—The lower end of the uterus, which is connected to the upper end of the vagina.

chancre—Sore caused by syphilis.

chlamydia—Very common bacterial STD.

condom—Thin sheath, or tube, usually made of latex, that is closed at one end and, when properly placed over the penis, keeps male fluid from entering the vagina. A female condom, inserted into the vagina, is open at the vagina and keeps male fluid from entering.

congenital syphilis—Syphilis acquired by a baby from its mother before or during birth.

discharge—Liquid that flows from a body opening. Some STDs have discharges from the penis or vagina.

ectopic pregnancy—The growth of a fertilized egg outside the uterus, often in the fallopian tube.

epidemic—Rapid spread of an infectious disease.

fallopian tubes—Passageways that carry eggs from the ovaries, where they are produced, to the uterus, where they can grow and be nourished properly.

genital warts—Viral STD caused by HPV that produces cauliflower-like growths in the genital area.

gonorrhea—Common bacterial STD that has been around for centuries.

hepatitis B—Highly contagious viral STD that attacks the liver and is spread through blood contact as well as sexual contact.

herpes simplex—Viral STD that produces sores.

Sexually Transmitted Diseases

human immunodeficiency virus (HIV)—Virus that attacks the immune system and eventually results in AIDS.

human papilloma virus (HPV)—One of several viruses that causes warts and, scientists believe, also causes cancer of the cervix.

immune system—Body system of white blood cells and other substances that fight infection.

incubation—Period of time between entry of a disease organism into the body and the appearance of symptoms of that disease.

infection—Harmful effects produced by a microbe that multiplies within the body.

infertility—Inability to conceive or bear children.

Kaposi's sarcoma—A cancer sometimes contracted by people with AIDS.

microbe—Another word for "microorganism."

microorganism—Life form too small to be seen except under a microscope.

mite—Very tiny eight-legged animal related to the spider.

organism—Life form.

pelvic inflammatory disease (PID)—Secondary infection, usually resulting from gonorrhea or chlamydia, that attacks a woman's fallopian tubes or uterus.

penicillin—First antibiotic drug ever discovered.

pubic lice—Tiny insects that infest the hair in the genital region and are thus transmitted sexually or by contact with infected clothing or bedding.

recurrence—Return of symptoms after having no symptoms for a period of time.

scabies—Extremely itchy STD caused by a mite that burrows under the skin.

sexually transmitted disease (STD)—Infection that is passed from one person to another primarily through sexual contact.

sterility—Inability to have children.

syphilis—Bacterial infection that is one of the oldest STDs.

venereal disease (VD)—An old term for STD.

Further Reading

Blake, Jeanne. *Risky Times: How to Be AIDS-Smart and Stay Healthy*. New York: Workman, 1990.

Curran, Christine Perdan. *Sexually Transmitted Diseases*. Springfield, N.J.: Enslow Publishers, Inc., 1998.

Daugirdas, John T. *STD: Sexually Transmitted Diseases, Including HIV/AIDS*. Hinsdale, Ill.: Medtext, 1992.

Johnson, Earvin "Magic." *What You Can Do to Avoid AIDS*. New York: Times Books, 1992.

Majure, Janet. *AIDS*. Springfield, N.J.: Enslow Publishers, Inc., 1992.

Nash, Carol Rust. *AIDS: Choices for Life*. Springfield, N.J.: Enslow Publishers, Inc., 1997.

National AIDS Clearinghouse, U.S. Department of Health and Human Services, Centers for Disease Control and Prevention, *AIDS Prevention Guide*. Rockville, Md.: n.d.

Nourse, Alan E. *Sexually Transmitted Diseases*. New York: Franklin Watts, 1992.

Thacker, John, Rachel Kranz, and Michael Bradman. *Straight Talk About Sexually Transmitted Diseases*. New York: Facts on File, 1993.

Woods, Samuel G. and Laura Diskavich. *Everything You Need to Know About STDs*. New York: Rosen Publishing Group, Inc., 1997.

A

abstinence, 51, 54
acquired immunodeficiency syndrome (AIDS), 8, 9, 13, 21, 22, 30, 42–44, 48
AIDS. *See* acquired immonodeficiency syndrome (AIDS).
alcohol, 16–17, 33, 52

B

bacteria, 8, 9–10, 22, 35, 36, 37, 47

C

chlamydia, 8, 9, 19, 24, 28, 37, 39
condom, 33, 51, 53–54
crabs. *See* pubic lice.

D

drinking. *See* alcohol.
drugs, illegal, 33, 42, 43, 52

G

genital warts, 8, 9, 22, 40–41, 46, 48, 54
gonorrhea, 8, 9, 19, 24, 28, 35, 37, 39, 51

H

hepatitis, 8, 9, 13, 22, 23, 42, 47, 48, 50
herpes, 8, 9, 22, 24–25, 26, 34, 39–40, 41, 45, 48, 54
HIV. *See* human immunodeficiency virus (HIV).
HPV. *See* human papilloma virus (HPV).
HSV. *See* herpes.
human immunodeficiency virus (HIV), 13, 21, 22, 23–24, 29, 42–44, 47, 48–49, 50. *See also* acquired immunodeficiency syndrome (AIDS).
human papilloma virus (HPV), 8, 9, 40–41, 46, 50

P

pelvic inflammatory disease (PID), 4, 8, 37–39
PID. *See* pelvic inflammatory disease (PID).
pregnancy, 15, 19, 22, 31, 32, 38–39, 51
pubic lice, 10, 12

S

scabies, 10, 12
sterility, 19, 35
syphilis, 8, 9, 22–23, 29, 35–37, 47

T

trichomoniasis, 10

V

virus, 8, 9, 10, 22, 23–25, 39–41, 42, 43–44, 46, 48, 50, 55

Henry County Library System
Locust Grove Public Library
P.O. Box 240, 3918 Highway 42
Locust Grove, GA 30248

LOCUST GROVE PUBLIC LIBRARY
115 LOCUST GROVE-GRIFFIN ROAD
LOCUST GROVE, GA 30248